Enter the Kin~dom

Studies in Luke and Acts

The first clue that the Gospel of Luke and the book of Acts were written by the same person lies in the opening lines of each book. The books of Luke and Acts were both written to Theophilus. The name Theophilus literally means "friend of God." Luke may have written to a Roman official who was a recent convert. Or he may have addressed Christians in general. We may never know to whom Luke originally addressed these books: a masterpiece of literary achievement that is Luke's Gospel, and the richly detailed history of the early church, the Acts of the Apostles. Taken together they continue to serve as a guide and challenge to all who are friends of God.

Luke's two books may be separated from each other by the Gospel of John in our Bibles, but for the writer of these two accounts, the drama of Acts builds on the story of Jesus in Luke. In Luke's first book, the author draws together written narratives and eyewitness stories of the life of Jesus to offer Theophilus "an orderly account… so that you may know the truth concerning the things about which you have been instructed." In his second book, Luke writes about what happened after the ascension of Jesus and the gift of the Holy Spirit.

The structure of these two books is much like a bow tie, moving from the wide end of the tie to the knot in the middle and broadening again at the other end. At the broad opening, Luke traces the genealogy of Jesus back to Adam (3:38) who is called "son of God," relating Jesus to all of humankind. But as the story of Jesus' life progresses, it focuses more and more on a very specific people—Hebrews in occupied Palestine. And at the very center of the account, Jesus is crucified and is buried. At the very end of Luke, Jesus is raised from the dead and appears to the women and other disciples. But that's not the end of the story. We're left hanging on a cliff until we get to Acts where Jesus' death and resurrection have planted the seeds for an enormous expansion of the faith.

Introduction

Acts begins in Jerusalem where we left off with Jesus, but it quickly takes us to much of the known world where Christianity has "caught on." Soon the story of faith has broadened out again to complete the shape of the bow tie. In each of the sessions in this unit, we will examine one broad theme in the ministry of Jesus that leads ultimately to the "central knot" of the cross and back out to Acts and the boundless growth of Christian discipleship.

As followers of Jesus, we are on the broad end of the story, led by the Holy Spirit to continue the expansion of Christ's ministry and infect the world with faith. What frontiers will we see? What new thing does God have in store for us? Let us be open to new possibilities so that we, like Peter, can say, "Who was I that I could hinder God?"

ABOUT THE WRITER

Bruce Yoder is on the staff of an urban retreat center in Richmond, Virginia. He has worked in pastoral ministry in the Mennonite Church.

Welcome to Good Ground!

Now that you know a little about the topic for this unit, let us introduce you to Good Ground, the series. Good Ground is a unique approach to Bible study. It lets the Bible ask most of the questions and lets participants struggle with the answers. When we ask, "How can I be saved?" the Bible asks, "Whom will you serve?" When we ask, "What will happen to me when I die?" the Bible asks, "What does the Lord require of you?" When we ask, "Whom does God love best?" the Bible asks, "Who is your neighbor?" Good Ground goes to the Scriptures for questions, not just answers.

Here's how each session is structured and what you can expect:

PART I: PREPARATION

We assume that you want to dig into Bible texts enough to do a little reading and thinking between sessions. In this section you are given the Bible passage(s) for the session, a key verse, a summary of the text and the issues it raises, and a three-page study on the text. The section concludes with "Things to think about," which offers some practical applications for everyday living.

We realize that in an age of prepackaged goods and 15-second sound bites, advance preparation may be a challenge. At the same time, we believe that for God's Word to be relevant to us, we need to do what it takes to ready our hearts and minds.

Part II: Session

Here we offer tips for your group when it meets, whether at church, in a home, or in some other setting. Good Ground uses a method for study that begins with everyday life (Focus), moves into an examination of what the Bible says (Engage the Text), then suggests life applications (Respond). The Closing wraps up the study in a brief worship experience.

One of the unique features about Good Ground studies is that they tap into a variety of learning styles. Some people learn best through the traditional lecture and discussion, but many others learn through visuals, imagination, poetry, role-playing, and the like. Through these varied learning experiences, Good Ground gets participants involved in the learning, moving beyond the head and into concrete living from the heart.

Part III: Leader Guidelines

We recognize that in many adult groups today, responsibility for leading is passed around within the group—hence the inclusion of notes for the leader in the participant's book. For these sessions to work best, however, those who lead must be prepared ahead of time. This section outlines what materials will be needed for the session, suggests some resources, and offers some tips for making the session come alive. If you are a regular leader of Good Ground, you will likely be aware of our other teaching/leading resources that orient you to our learning philosophy and methods.

Enjoy working with Good Ground as you journey in your faith, growing to be more like Christ!

>Julie Garber, editor
>Byron Rempel-Burkholder, editor
>Ken Hawkley, adult education consultant

Session 1

Jesus Who?

PART I: PREPARATION

Bible passages: Luke 9:18-20; Acts 2:22-40

Key verse: He said to them, "But who do you say that I am?" Peter answered, "The Messiah of God" (Luke 9:20).

Summary: This passage in Luke is pivotal. To this point Jesus has been traveling widely in the countryside of Galilee, ministering to a wide variety of communities there. But when Peter declares that Jesus is the Messiah, Jesus immediately begins to focus on a return to Jerusalem and on the future of suffering he will face there at the hands of his own people. Jews had dreamed of a messiah who would save them. They longed for someone to appear to end their repression and reestablish God's people again. However, as Peter points out in Acts 2, it is the Jews who allow Jesus the Messiah to be killed. Whom did Jesus come to save? Who are God's people? Is God's salvation for everyone? Would we recognize the Messiah today?

Study

"Who do you say that I am?" That was the pointed question Jesus asked Peter. It is a question that is just as appropriate for us today. Who was Jesus two thousand years ago? Who is Jesus today?

The Jews of Jesus' time waited for the Messiah, God's Chosen One, God's Anointed One, who would usher in the realm of God. The work of Luke-Acts was the writer's attempt to put into perspective for the early church just who Jesus was and how his messiahship fit the history of messianic expectations in the older Hebrew scriptures. Jesus' question, "Who do you say that I am," brings into sharp focus the uncertainty and conflict over expectations of who the messiah would be and what the messiah would do.

Though Jesus formed the church from a few Jewish followers, most Jews did not believe that Jesus was God's Chosen One. To these doubtful Jews, Luke tries to show that Jesus was (and is) the one for whom Israel waited. He was and is the divine/human agent who offers salvation to all who are in need. He invites people to live as God's people in God's "kindom" or realm. How he offered that invitation apparently made sense to some but not to others.

What is a messiah?
Some Jews sought a kingly messiah who would rule the political as well as the religious world. In Psalm 2, the newly anointed king is described thus: "You are my son; today I have begotten you." In Hebrew, *anointed* is literally "messiah." Anointing is also at the root of the Greek word "Christ." Jesus Christ is Jesus the Anointed One or Jesus the Messiah.

> When Oscar Romero fed the poor, people said he was a saint. When he asked why people were poor, people called him a communist.

Luke's picture of Jesus as the Messiah certainly has this royal dimension. Notice that when Jesus rises out of the baptismal waters in Luke 3:22, God says, "You are my Son, the Beloved; with you I am well pleased." Like a king, God is handing over authority to a first son. But in this case the heir is not just a blood relative. God chooses Jesus and proclaims Jesus to be the son, the anointed heir, almost as if by adoption. Already we have a clue that this Messiah will be different from what the people are expecting.

In Hebrew scriptures, the kingly messiah is more than an autocrat, ruling with a righteous hand. He has special responsibilities to maintain justice, especially for the poor. Jesus picked up this theme in his first sermon (Luke 4:18-19). However, many first-century Jews, whose homeland was occupied by the Roman army, thought of a kingly messiah as primarily a military leader. Salvation would come through "our" domination and violence that would defeat "their" domination and violence.

In addition to the royal Son who is a "kingly messiah," Luke also paints Jesus as a "prophetic messiah." The prophets in the Hebrew scriptures are the ones who persistently link religious practice with concrete acts of justice. Though the royal or "kingly messiah" would push for justice, he is primarily associated with political power. The "prophetic messiah," on the other hand, continually stands over against power, issuing a clarion call for social reform. When Israel tended the altar of God with utmost care and concern but failed to treat the aliens among them with hospitality or the poor with justice or the widows with mercy, the prophets raised their voices.

Jesus Who?

> Jerusalem is the "knot in the bow tie" in Luke's Gospel. Luke refers to Jerusalem 90 times; the entire remainder of the New Testament includes only 49 references to Jerusalem.

The prophetic messiah stood in the line of Isaiah (cf. Isa. 58:6-12), Amos (cf. Amos 5:21-24), and Micah (cf. Micah 6:6-8). Here salvation comes through challenges to the legalistic and sometimes corrupt religious system in order to help the poor, including in Luke all who are on the margins of the community of faith, such as women, the poor, the sick, tax collectors, prostitutes, and children. In this case, salvation is a sort of social reform. Jews who expected a kingly messiah were united in seeing the enemy as an outside force trying to destroy Judaism. But the school that believed in the prophetic messiah was self-critical, identifying decay within the community and calling Jews themselves to accountability in order to be saved.

From Isaiah we get yet another view of a messiah, that of the suffering servant (42:1-4; 50:4-11; 53:1-5). The suffering servant will take onto him or herself the sins of the world in order to save it from judgment. In many ways, Jesus also fits this description of a messiah, though few people were convinced that salvation would come either through repentance or suffering.

These messianic expectations were, and are, like lenses through which we see Jesus and his mission to the world. In a situation of political oppression, it was difficult for first-century Jews to see God's Messiah as a suffering servant whose prophetic message was directed not toward the external enemy, but toward internal corruption. Yet, this is, above the others, the type of messiah that Luke says Jesus was—and is.

Who am I?

Jesus asks Peter, "Who do you say that I am?" Peter declares that Jesus is the Messiah. We don't know immediately what kind of messiah Peter thinks Jesus is. Perhaps Peter himself didn't know at that point. It wasn't until after his denial of Jesus, the crucifixion, and resurrection that Peter preached a sermon that reveals Jesus as the *crucified and risen* Jesus who is both Lord and Messiah (Acts 2:22-36). Jesus brought judgment like a prophet and suffered for the very people he condemned.

The suffering Messiah stands at the center of Luke's story both in his Gospel and in Acts. In characteristic fashion, the identity of Jesus at first is broad—named only "the Anointed One," whatever that means. By the end of the Gospel, the messiahship of Jesus is more narrowly defined as that of a Suffering Servant. Here is the narrow knot of the bow tie. But the identity of Jesus then broadens again in Acts where the Suffering Servant becomes the Savior of not only Jews but of Gentiles as well—"everyone whom the Lord our God calls to him" (Acts 2:39).

While Luke's picture of Jesus becomes ever clearer as we move through the two books, "Who do you say that I am?" is still a question worth asking. When we formulate a response, it is also worth naming our own expectations of the messiah. Do we want a kingly messiah who will have power and control? Are we looking for a prophetic messiah who addresses social injustice not only in the lives of others, but in our lives as well? What about a priestly messiah who will reform the religious practices of today? What about a suffering messiah in a world filled with violence? Naming our expectations up front will help us be honest about how we relate to Jesus and how we will function as the body of Christ, commissioned to be Christ for the world, carrying on his ministry.

Things to think about: Make a checklist for yourself. On a slip of paper write the words *government, poverty, worship, service*. Think about what a messiah could do in each case to save or reform each one. Which one do you believe Jesus came to do primarily? Talk to others at home, work, or school this week about their views.

> To the Christian the Jew is the incomprehensibly obdurate man, who declines to see what has happened; and to the Jew the Christian is the incomprehensibly daring man, who affirms in an unredeemed world that its redemption has been accomplished.
>
> —Martin Buber, *The Word*

Part II: Session

Focus (10 minutes)

After announcements, offering, sharing, prayer, or other preliminary class activities, choose one of the following options to focus your thinking as a group.

Option A: Fashion a bow tie. On a piece of paper, draw a big bow tie. Use your drawing as a chart for your life, your education, your work, or other facet of life. How, in each of these, did you work toward a specific focus and then broaden your view? Work alone for a few minutes and then come back together to share your charts.

Transition: The ministry of Jesus as told in Luke and Acts takes the shape of a bow tie. In his early ministry, Jesus ministers to a broad range

Jesus Who?

> There is no consensus among scholars about the nature of the term "Son of Man." It may refer to the apocalyptic figure in Daniel who signaled the beginning of a new age. Or, it may be a polite Aramaic way of referring to oneself as a "child of humanity." In the first case it is a title; in the second it is not.

of people, then turns his attention to Jerusalem and the Jews alone. In Acts the apostles carry on his work, taking the gospel from Jerusalem and the Jews out into the world. Look at the text to see why the Messiah, who was sent to the Jews, cares so much for outsiders.

Option B: Would you know Jesus if you saw him? Quickly jot down on a card the end of this sentence: If the Messiah returned today, I would probably know by_____ . (Name characteristics of the Messiah as you think they would appear today.) Put your card in a pile and draw out someone else's. Read the anonymous cards to each other. How similar or different are the expectations today about the Messiah?

Transition statement: Just as we hold different understandings of who the messiah would be today, so, too, did the men and women of first-century Palestine. Explore Luke and Acts to see why there was so much confusion about the Savior.

Option C: Take a group vote. Designate corners of the room as "government," "the church," "social injustice," and "voluntary service." Cast your vote by standing in the area that you believe Jesus would most likely return to fix. When all voters are in place, make some observations about where the most votes are located and how each area ranks after the first.

Transition: Probably the majority of Jews expected a kingly messiah, a ruler and general, who would overthrow the Roman occupation army. But that's not what happened. Look at Luke and Acts to see why God did the unexpected.

Engage the Text (25 MINUTES)

Option A: Geography of a bow tie. Divide into two groups, one for Luke and one for Acts. In 10 minutes, quickly note the geographical location of Jesus or the apostles in each chapter of the book. Come back together and trace the journey of the Gospel on a Bible times map. What generalizations can you make about Jesus' ministry based on geography? How is Jesus' route like a bow tie?

Option B: Who says what about Jesus? Divide into three small groups. Group 1 will read Luke 4:16-21, 31-37. Group 2 will read Luke 7:16, 39-40 and Luke 9:7-20, 35. Group 3 will read Luke 19:37-40 and Luke 23:35-38. Be prepared to report back to the whole group a definition of *messiah* based on your Bible verses. As a whole group, talk about why the perceptions are so varied. Why didn't God supply a straightforward, plain-speaking definition of a messiah?

Option C: Listen up! Listen as someone in the group delivers Peter's sermon to the Jews in Acts 2 as a real sermon or dramatic reading. Then discuss two things: If Jews are the oppressed, why is Peter chastising them? And who did Jesus come to save, according to Peter? Just who was "everyone whom the Lord our God calls"?

Respond (10 MINUTES)

Option A: Ask the question today. Grapple with Jesus' first question: "Who do people say that I am? Answer it for today. Then respond to Jesus' second question: "Who do you say that I am?" Answer it for yourselves. If it is difficult to share personally in the large group, consider breaking into small groups of two or three people. And, if necessary, sit in silence for a minute or two to reflect before answering.

Option B: Jesus came for "all." Peter says that Jesus came for "everyone whom the Lord our God calls." Talk about who God calls today. To what extent does God call Christians? To what extent does God call outsiders? Where do Jews fit in the work of salvation today? Muslims? Hindus? others?

Option C: Repent! Peter tells the Jews not to worry. They can still be part of the plan. In pairs, talk about how you personally need to repent or change in order to be part of God's plan of saving grace in this world. Make a plan with your PEP (Partners Encouraging Perseverance) to change in one small way in the coming weeks. Agree to a schedule for checking on one another's progress by visits, phone conversations, or e-mail messages.

Closing (5 MINUTES)

Gather in a circle. Tie a knot in the middle of a sturdy paper napkin or handkerchief. Hold your bow ties by the knot and pray for the church and the head of the church, Jesus Christ. Take turns praying aloud for the church. Then hold the bow tie by the wide end. Take turns again, this time praying aloud for the world in need of a messiah.

Part III: Leader Guidelines

Items Needed
Paper
Pens
Index cards
Dinner napkins or handkerchiefs for each participant
Bibles
Bible map of the New Testament

Resources
Green, Joel B. *The Gospel of Luke* (New International Commentary). Eerdmans, 1997.

Kraybill, Donald. *The Upside-Down Kingdom*, rev. ed. Herald Press, 1990.

Pelikan, Jaroslav. *The Illustrated Jesus Through the Centuries*. Yale University Press, 1997.

A video of the life of Jesus.

Tips for Leading
1. Read the entire unit before you begin leading. Introduce the unit by summarizing the introduction. Let people know about PEPs (Partners Encouraging Perseverance) and any other ways they can be prepared for study.
2. Ask participants to respect confidentiality in small group sharing. People will feel freer to share deeply if they trust that information will not be shared outside the group.
3. Draw out quiet participants in discussion. Ask more vocal people to refrain from responding until others who wish have spoken.
4. When posing quesions to the group, phrase them in such a way that they cannot be answered yes or no. You will engender more discussion if participants must articulate a full response.
5. Encourage participants to choose a partner to be a PEP. Suggest that partners draw names from a hat to avoid pairing up with close friends.

Session 2
Healing the Broken, Breaking the Status Quo

Part I: Preparation

Bible passages: Luke 6:6-11; 9:1-2; Acts 16:16-34

Key verse: Then Jesus called the twelve together and gave them power and authority over all demons and to cure diseases, and he sent them out to proclaim the kingdom of God and to heal (Luke 9:1-2).

Summary: In Luke 9, Jesus commissions the 12 disciples and sends them out to do two things: to proclaim the kingdom of God and to heal. In the story in Luke of the man healed on the Sabbath and the story of Paul healing the servant girl in Acts, proclamation and healing happen in the same action. To proclaim the kingdom is to throw down the barriers and reconcile people to each other and to God. To heal them is to bind up their physical wounds and end their alienation from God and from the people, restoring them to the faith community. But when Jesus reconciles people and makes them whole, he stirs up a great deal of conflict. Why did the prospect of new life and wholeness threaten the status quo in Jesus' time? To what extent do claims of wholeness and new life in Christ threaten the status quo today? To what extent should it be more of a threat than it already is?

Study

The topic of healing is complex, as it should be, for life is complex. Health is not easily defined in physiological terms without also considering the mind and the spirit. Moreover, health and wholeness may be affected by events of the past, and circumstances of the present may affect future health and wholeness. A factory closing in a community in

Healing the Broken, Breaking the Status Quo

the past might be manifested today in the bruises and broken bones of a beaten spouse. Child abuse within a family a generation ago might affect the present generation. The current stress in a congregation, causing unresolved conflicts, may find expression in the months ahead in the back problems experienced by the pastor.

Adding to the complexity of healing is that it is never enough for one person to be healed individually. Healing affects everyone who is connected to a sick person. When a child is made well, the whole family is relieved of disease. When a co-worker is healed, a whole staff is restored to completeness. When a member of a congregation gets well, the faith community becomes whole again. Not only are our bodies in need of healing. So, too, are relationships, families, and even institutions.

> Healing narratives make up fully one-fifth of the Gospels! The healing that Jesus brought left people not just cured but "whole"—restored to God and to their faith community.

For Luke, healing is a process in all these respects—body, mind, and spirit. But more than anything, perhaps, healing, for Luke, is to restore relationships. When Jesus sends the 12 out with the command to proclaim the good news of God's reign, the only other specific command is to heal (Luke 9:1-2). That these two commands are linked says something about both the nature of God's reign and the nature of healing. Judging from the healing stories, Luke believes the kingdom, or what may more appropriately be called the "kin-dom," is the faith community reconciled to itself and to God.

Within the healing stories in Luke and Acts, God does not act arbitrarily, healing this one or that one. Nor do God's healing acts always depend on the faith of a person. Rather, Luke portrays God at work through Jesus, breaking down barriers of division and inviting people back into the faith community. Healing may include bodily cure, but the fundamentals of healing have more to do with the restoration of rightful relationships within God's community of faith and with God.

Jesus was not the only healer of his day. Other people healed, as well. What distinguishes the healing events in Luke and Acts is the repeated accounting of relationships that are restored among people and between individuals and God. The other distinguishing characteristic of these stories is that each incident of healing sparks a conflict between Christians and those who prefer the status quo.

Consider the following multi-dimensional healing stories in Luke:

Luke 6:6-11: Healing on the Sabbath was a serious offense, technically punishable by death if it occurred after a warning. Jesus boldly heals a man on the Sabbath, pointing out that Jewish leaders distort the law against "working on the Sabbath." In Jesus' mind, healing is not work but restoration, precisely the thing for which the law was made. The Sabbath was made to allow people to restore and rejuvenate themselves after six days of work. For leaders to prohibit healing on the Sabbath is the greater offense.

Luke 8:26-39: When Jesus crosses the Sea of Galilee to the Gentile land of the Gerasenes, he meets "a man of the city" (v. 27) who has demons, living among the tombs. When the man is healed, he is restored in two ways. He is restored to "his right mind" (v. 35), or physically, and he is restored to his home in the city (v. 39), or relationally. Predictably, this double restoration is met with fear and suspicion from the locals (v. 37).

> Are any among you suffering? They should pray. Are any cheerful? They should sing songs of praise. Are any among you sick? They should call for the elders of the church and have them pray over them, anointing them with oil in the name of the Lord. The prayer of faith will save the sick, and the Lord will raise them up; and anyone who has committed sins will be forgiven. Therefore confess your sins to one another, and pray for one another, so that you may be healed. The prayer of the righteous is powerful and effective.
>
> James 5:13-16.

Luke 8:40-56. Right in the middle of the story of the girl who is restored to life, we take a side trip to the healing story of the woman with hemorrhages who is ritually unclean and cast out of the Jewish community. Not only is she ritually unclean and a woman, she violates the law by touching Jesus. No woman, especially one who was ritually unclean, dared touch a rabbi. She does. Yet she is restored to health and to the community. On either side of her story is that of a leader of the synagogue whose daughter has died. Daughters of Abraham had less standing in the culture of Jesus than sons of Abraham, yet she too is restored. Might Luke have placed these two stories together to emphasize Jesus' concern for females who were as much children of God as males? In any case, they are both healed in a relational sense as much as they are healed physically. Defying the social and religious code at times like these put Jesus as odds with Jewish leaders who struggled to keep the faith intact under occupation.

Luke 17:11-19. More than a physical ailment, leprosy carried a strong social and religious stigma that separated those who had the ailment from those who did not. People with leprosy were required to ring a bell when another person approached so that the passerby would know to avoid the unclean person in the path. People skirted even the shadow of someone with leprosy, believing even the shadow could contaminate.

In a region between Samaria and Galilee (which is no-man's-land, for Samaritans and Jews would have nothing to do with each other), a band of 10 lepers, one Samaritan and nine Jews, are bound together at the margins of their respective communities by their shared illness. Following the physical cure only the Samaritan leper recognizes that he has also been restored relationally to God. Jesus tells the man, as some translations render verse 19, "your faith has saved you." If that is so, then salvation is healing beyond the body; it is the practice of community medicine through the restoration of a right relationship with God and among people.

> Come, Holy Spirit, that is in creation,
>   come to repair our worn and tired souls;
> Come, Holy Spirit, that is in healing,
>   come to bind our bent and bruised bodies;
> Come, Holy Spirit, that is in thought,
>   come to refresh our patterned and crusted minds;
> Come, Holy Spirit, that is in our spirits,
>   come to live in us and inspire us. Amen.
>
> —Leland Wilson, adapt. (*For All Who Minister*, a Worship Manual for the Church of the Brethren)

The bow tie

The theme of healing and restoration in Luke and Acts fits handily in the bow tie structure outlined in the first session. In session 1, we saw how Jesus' ministry started broadly, like the end of a bow tie, and then narrowed to the knot of a bow tie with a focus on Jews in the seat of Jewish power, Jerusalem. In Acts, the ministry of the apostles broadens out again to reach Gentiles as well as Jews, and presumably the "ends of the earth."

Healing stories also take the shape of the bow tie in Luke's writings. At first we encounter Jesus healing many people on his route through Galilee and as he heads toward Jerusalem, but the healing stories of Luke come to their real climax at the cross. The cross stands at the center of the bow tie. In Jesus on the cross, God shares our suffering and offers healing. We may suffer from physical pain caused by sickness or accident. We may struggle with being ostracized for violating social norms. We may be alienated from others by chronic depression or mental illness. We may labor under the weight of sin that is unconfessed. In all its forms, pain isolates us, but whatever the pain, God suffers with us. We are not alone. We are being healed by God's presence in our lives, reconciling us and making us whole. This is the ministry that Jesus' disciples took on for themselves, going out into the world to reconcile others to Christ. All pain and alienation led Jesus to the narrow cross. And Jesus on the cross led his followers to a wide ministry of healing.

A healing ministry
Here are two of many examples of how the ministry of Jesus was carried on by the early church. In Acts 3:1-10, Peter and John heal a man lame from birth. After they minister to him, he is able to enter the temple as a fellow worshiper rather than a social outcast. He is restored to full membership in the community.

In Acts 16:16-24, Paul heals a young slave girl in Philippi with a spirit of divination. By doing so, they deprive her owners of their livelihood made from her fortune-telling. This is a bold example of Christians standing up to economic exploitation and the powerful objections of the public when their pocketbooks are threatened. In this case it's not just Jewish authorities who are up in arms. Gentiles are after Paul and Silas, claiming that Paul and Silas are "disturbing our city" (v. 20).

When Paul and Silas heal the woman with a spirit of divination, they free her from her social relationship as slave to master. Without the spirit of divination, she is no longer exploitable. She no longer has value as a slave but as a full human being. The people who object to the healing have well-founded fears that this sort of belief could upset the whole institution of slavery and should be quashed.

As long as the status quo leaves some people at the margins of society or stigmatized or exploited for the gain of others, the ministry of healing will bring reconciliation for some and turmoil for others. If the social order isn't shaken up once in a while, it may be because there is no healing going on and we have fallen down in the ministry that Christ gave us to do. Think of it—our part is simple. Jesus took the pain of the world on himself to reconcile us to God. We don't have to suffer under horrible alienation. All we have to do is proclaim the "kin-dom" and live it wholly.

Things to think about: Make a chronicle of your health—spiritual, physical, and relational—over your lifetime. In your experience, how do the body and soul relate?

This week engage people with whom you live, work, and worship in conversation about healing. Try to define healing for yourself and ask others to do the same. How do you think healing happens? To what extent is it a miracle? a ministry? What do you make of faithful people who pray for physical healing but never get well physically? Do you think God acts against the laws of nature to cure physical illness?

PART II: SESSION

Focus (15 MINUTES)

After the opening of the class, choose one of the following options to focus on the theme for this session.

Option A: Take your congregation's temperature. Divide into groups of four or five people. If you have a small group, give your opinions individually. Decide together how healthy or how ill your congregation is. What is its temperature? What are its symptoms? What name would you give the illness? What would you prescribe? Choose a spokesperson to report your findings to the larger group.

Option B: In groups of three or four, go through the circulars in a Sunday paper and find every advertisement you can related to health and healing. Look for coupons for health products; promises of younger skin, more hair; miracle vitamins; and foolproof diet plans. What parts of the body seem to receive the most focus? What parts of the body still need attention? As a group, come up with a "medicine" for what ails society. Give your product a name and share it with the larger group.

Transition: Health and healing have many dimensions, not the least of which has to do with healthy relationships to God and others. What is true about healing today was true for the people of first-century Palestine. Let's turn to two healing stories: Luke 17:11-19 and Acts 16:16-24.

Option C: Use playing cards to make a "house of cards." See whose house stands the longest. After the competition, talk about how a house of cards is like the status quo in society. How close are we at any time to social structures collapsing? What keeps them intact? What might cause social institutions to fall?

Session 2

Transition: Jesus' healing ministry upset the status quo. The status quo, of course, is usually defined by people who benefit from the way things are. Look at stories of healing in Luke and Acts to find out what the status quo of Jesus' time was and how it did or didn't change.

Engage the Text (20 MINUTES)

Option A: Rewrite the stories. In small groups, rewrite the story of the 10 lepers. Substitute a social group akin to the Samaritans today and a social disease akin to leprosy. Read your versions of this parable for each other. Then rewrite the story of the slave girl with a spirit of divination. What exploited group might she represent today? Who might exploit her condition? Where in the world might Paul and Silas be if the story were told today? Read your versions of this story to each other.

Option B: Track the changes in the status quo. Listen as a volunteer reads aloud the story of the 10 lepers in Luke 17:11-19. Use a commentary or study Bible to answer the following questions about the status quo or "the way things were."
1. What was the long-standing conflict between Jews and Samaritans?
2. Why did lepers keep their distance?
3. Why did Jesus tell them to "go and show yourselves to the priests"?
4. Why do you think the nine Jews ran off without saying thank you?
5. What would our society look like today if the status quo then were the status quo now?

Listen as a volunteer reads the story in Acts about the slave girl with the spirit of divination (Acts 16:16-34). Then discuss the following questions about the status quo in the Bible.
1. Why do you suppose the religious community tolerated slavery in Paul's time?
2. What is a spirit of divination? Is there anything like it today?
3. In what way are Paul and Silas "disturbing our city" by doing a good deed for the slave girl?
4. Should the public be allowed to help police catch and punish suspects as they do in verse 22? Why or why not?
5. Why does the jailer decide to kill himself in verse 27?
6. At what point would you change the status quo?

Option C: Illustrate the stories. Divide into two groups. One group will illustrate the story of the 10 lepers in comic strip fashion. The other group will illustrate the story of the slave girl with a spirit of divination in comic strip fashion. Choose a spokesperson from your group to present your group's comic strip to the whole group. Post the stories for all to see. In the large group, compare the two stories. How are the healing stories alike? How are they different? Does the conflict that arises in each case produce change? How is the change in the status quo for the good?

Respond (10 MINUTES)

Option A: Tell stories. Share in a small group or with the whole group about a time your faith made you feel more whole. At the same time, how did your faith put you at odds with the community or society? What did others stand to lose by your healing and becoming whole?

Option B: Minister to a local situation. Decide where in your community there is the greatest need for reconciliation. Identify who stands to lose and who stands to gain by reconciliation in this instance. Brainstorm how you as a group could help reconciliation happen. If possible, carry out a plan for facilitating reconciliation. Or talk about what keeps you from being an instrument of reconciliation at times. Why is it hard to rock the boat?

Option C: Identify an area of alienation within your own life. Share with your PEP or in a small group how alienation affects your spirit, your physical health, and your relationships. Listen to the suggestions of others about how healing might take place, and examine any resistance you may feel to their suggestions. Covenant with your PEP to work on this problem in the coming week.

Closing (5 MINUTES)

Sing together "There is a Balm in Gilead." Stand in a circle and lay your left hand on the shoulder of the person beside you. Pray in silence for the healing of the person you are touching.

PART III: LEADER GUIDELINES

Items Needed
Sheets of paper
Colored pencils, crayons, or markers
Tape
Sunday paper circulars
Deck of playing cards

Tips for Leading

1. Be aware that many people have unspoken pains and feelings of alienation from the faith community. People may be more willing to share deeply during the session if they share in small groups of one or two other people.
2. Begin the session by asking the group to respect the views and experiences of individuals in the group. Some may have personal experiences of the miraculous and others may have little faith in miracles. The first healing of the day may be the willingness of all to honor the experiences of others, even when they are very different from their own.
3. During the session opening, check with the group to see how the PEP partners are feeling. Was the initial contact useful? Does it help to have a partner for accountability? How easy is it to talk with a new friend?
4. It may be useful in discussion to find out if the group considers itself part of the status quo or in tension with the status quo. What good connotations and what bad connotations does this term have for the group?

Session 3

Welcome, Neighbor: Gospel Hospitality

Part I: Preparation

Bible passages: Luke 7:36-50; Acts 11:1-18

Key verse: If then God gave them the same gift that he gave us when we believed in the Lord Jesus Christ, who was I that I could hinder God? (Acts 11:17).

Summary: Two stories of hospitality, one in Luke and one in Acts, demonstrate the broad invitation to become part of the household of God. In Luke 7:36-50, a disreputable woman scandalizes a Pharisee by extending hospitality to Jesus in the customary way, by bathing the dusty feet of her household guest. In Acts, Peter, the impeccable Jew, violates Jewish dietary law to accept the hospitality of Gentiles. In both stories, it is the outsider who wishes to belong to the family of God and extends hospitality to the faithful. The faithful do a new thing by accepting the hospitality of sinners and Gentiles, witnessing to the welcome God offers everyone. How can we, like the Pharisee and Peter, turn our homes and the church, our spiritual refuge, into places of welcome for the people God forgives and invites inside?

Study

In Jewish custom of Jesus' day, a shared meal symbolized a shared life. When you ate with someone, it was a statement of unity and intimacy. When the Pharisee invites Jesus to a meal, it indicates that the Pharisee accepts Jesus, that they are of the same mind. However, when Jesus allows the sinful woman to anoint his feet, the Pharisee assumes Jesus has misjudged and that perhaps Jesus is not a prophet.

Suspecting that the Pharisee is annoyed, Jesus uses a parable to cleverly turn the Pharisee's rule for exclusion into a rule for inclusion. In Luke, Jesus uses many parables in this fashion, opening the invitation of the Gospel to a host of outcasts, women, and sinners largely from Jesus' own culture and community—that is, they are Hebrew outcasts, women, and sinners. Later in Acts, this invitation will be extended beyond even Jews to include Gentiles from the ends of the earth.

We can learn a lot about Jesus' radical invitation by looking at the parables. In fact, three of his most enduring and endearing parables were given in response to the very inhospitable charge: "This fellow welcomes sinners and even eats with them." The three parables are those of a found sheep, a found coin, and a found young man, more commonly referred to as the parables of the Lost Sheep, the Lost Coin, and the Prodigal Son (Luke 15:1-32). While dining with a Pharisee named Simon, Jesus tells another parable in response to the unspoken judgment leveled against the woman who kissed the feet of Jesus and bathed them with her tears (Luke 7:36-50). One of the things we learn from this parable is that Jesus came not for the faithful, but for the sinner. But one of the most surprising things we learn is that, as much as we'd like to identify with Jesus in this story, we are more often like the Pharisee in the text for today or the older brother who resents the warm welcome his prodigal brother receives.

> God is a circle whose center is everywhere and whose circumference is nowhere.
>
> —St. Augustine

This ministry of hospitality in Luke is one side (and a major emphasis) of our by now famous bow tie. At the knot of the bow tie is, again, the cross, which Jesus endures to open the way for others to have faith, even offering forgiveness to sinners on the cross next to him. Oddly, Peter, who should know better, has denied knowing Jesus, and the women who served him stand back from the cross in an inhospitable distancing of themselves from Jesus. Even Israelite criminals denounce Jesus on the cross. Only the Roman centurion recognizes Jesus for who he is and proclaims Jesus' innocence. His gesture foreshadows the months to come when the whole ministry of the church will turn outward to the world of non-Jews.

Peter reports
Acts is a bridge between two worlds—all of Jewish history and the church of Jesus Christ. The preachers in Acts—Peter, Stephen, and

Welcome, Neighbor: Gospel Hospitality

> That ceremonies prescribed in the Law are no longer practiced is not a result of a command, but is a freedom permitted by love.
>
> —Hans Denck, "Concerning True Love" in Early Anabaptist Spirituality

Paul—stand in the middle of the bridge helping people of faith cross over from the shore of Israelite history and tradition to the new shore of the church. In their sermons they trace a trajectory of Israelite history that leads inevitably to Jesus and then beyond Israelite history to a faith that is wide open for those who believe. For instance, Stephen's speech to the high priest of the temple in Jerusalem in Acts 7 retells the story of Israel from its early stages, culminating in the life and ministry of Jesus the Messiah. Stephen's special vantage point is that he is Greek, a Hellenistic Jew and not Hebrew. When he speaks of "our ancestor Abraham" (v. 2) and "our people in Egypt" (v. 17), he is already pushing Judaism beyond bloodlines.

At the Pentecostal outpouring of the Spirit in Acts 2, the good news of Jesus is shared in a variety of languages, underscoring the expansive grace of God. It is for everyone. All are unified and welcome in God's family despite differences and shortcomings. But that warm hospitality was not an easy lesson to learn, especially for Peter, who was a Hebrew and a very devout Jew, committed to the survival of Judaism through ritual purity. To this point, Peter has led an exemplary life, keeping the commandments and living according to the law. His rigorous practice of Judaism makes his story about crossing the bridge all the more remarkable.

Peter's sermon in Acts 11 is addressed to fellow Jewish Christians (Acts 11) who think much like Peter used to think. They criticize him for going to uncircumcised men (Gentiles) and eating unclean food with them. To them he is threatening to kill the faith by making it too easy, too popular. This becomes the crux of the problem. Does one have to be Jewish and undergo circumcision and purification, that is, become a Jew, in order to be a follower of Christ? At one point Peter may have thought so, but when the Holy Spirit directs him to accept non-Jews, he cannot refuse: "If then God gave them the same gift that he gave us when we believed in the Lord Jesus Christ, who was I that I could hinder God?" (Acts 11:17). He no longer believes it is necessary to seal the covenant with God with physical circumcision, but with a circumcision of the heart, in other words, with a commitment made from within.

Before we condemn the high priest and other Jews, including Jewish Christians, in these stories, we must remember that the issues they dealt with are still the ones we wrestle with today. When we think of an evangelistic program or opening the church to new members, we usually think of attracting nice families, hard workers, and people pretty much like us. We rarely think of drawing in strangers, outsiders, people very much unlike us. Even when we're not campaigning for new members, our churches can tend to be clubs, excluding people without the right qualifications. We don't do it intentionally, but like the unsuspecting Pharisee, we like the message of Jesus until it hits too close to home. Or like Peter, we worry that accepting people who are less than perfect will contaminate the body or weaken it. If we lower our standards and take in criminals and sinners, what will happen to our church? Will outsiders take the gospel as seriously as we do? If we let them in, are we condoning their behavior? If new people come in, do we have to give up our favorite hymns, our traditions, and our style of worship?

> The congregation which takes seriously biblical understanding of hospitality does not place restrictions on its welcome and actively seeks out those whom others might overlook.
>
> —from *Widening the Welcome of Your Church* by Fred Bernhard and Steve Clapp

Jesus opened the faith to the imperfect, the outcast, the powerless of Judaism. And the Holy Spirit opened the faith up to any, Jew and Gentile alike, with a circumcised heart. This being so, "who was I that I could hinder God?"

Things to think about: Sit down with a congregational directory this week. Look at the names in the directory and inventory the wide range of gifts and commitments of the people you worship with. Think especially hard about those with whom you have little in common, or even those for whom you have little respect. Pray a prayer of thanksgiving for them.

Consider offering a meal to a small group of people you would not normally associate with, such as people of another culture, economic background, or religious faith. Or pair up with another member of your group and plan the meal together.

Part II: The Session

Focus (10 minutes)
After the usual opening activities, choose one of the following options to focus on the session.

Welcome, Neighbor: Gospel Hospitality

Option A: Recall awkward moments. Tell about the most awkward experience you have ever had as either a host or a guest in someone's home. When everyone who wants to has had a chance to tell a story, talk briefly about what makes you feel awkward in social settings, such as poor manners or associating with people with whom you have nothing in common.

Option B: Open the door. Take turns opening the door to the room where you are meeting to the degree to which you feel the church is hospitable to strangers and outsiders. When it is your turn, give a brief explanation for why you think the church is welcoming or exclusive.

Option C: Examine yourself. On a piece of paper, write a large letter *T* if you are a person who likes tradition or a large letter *C* if you are a person who likes change. Take turns telling why you chose the letter you chose. For a variation on this exercise, write the letter *L* if you like to socialize mostly with people who are like you or *U* if you like to socialize with a variety of people who are unlike you. Take turns telling why you chose the letter you chose.

> It does not say anywhere in the Torah to invite your guest to pray; but it [the Torah] does require us to offer food, drink, and a bed.
>
> "The Chofetz Chaim," quoted in *The Word*

Transition: Often we think of the church as a refuge where we can worship with like-minded people, our closest friends with whom we can truly be ourselves. This is where we feel most at home. We even talk about having a "church home" where we, like Jesus, retreat to the familiarity and comfort of a small band of fellow worshipers. But Jesus also gave and accepted hospitality in many unlikely places from unlikely people. Despite his deep friendship with the disciples, they did not make up the church. The church for Jesus is something else. See how Jesus and Peter define the church in Luke and Acts.

Engage the Text (20 MINUTES)

Option A: Divide into two groups, one to study Luke 7:36-50 and one to study Acts 11:1-18. Listen as the story is read aloud to your group.
Group 1 discussion questions (Luke 7:36-50):
1. Name all the characters who offer hospitality in this story. What shock value does each have as a host?
2. What, if anything, does it tell us about Jesus only accepting hospitality, but never offering it in this story?
3. According to this story, how can we show hospitality to God? How does God show hospitality to people?

Session 3

4. Look up *hospitality* in a Bible dictionary. How important was hospitality to strangers in Judaism? As a keeper of tradition, why do you suppose the Pharisee didn't seem to know about rules of hospitality?
5. Choose a reporter who can recap the responses to these questions for the large group.

Group 2 discussion questions (Acts 11:1-18):
1. If Peter went against Jewish dietary codes recorded in scripture, to what extent must we follow biblical teachings?
2. If the Holy Spirit and the scriptures teach different things, which should people obey? Why?
3. How did Peter know that God, and not temptation, was speaking, telling him to eat forbidden food?
4. How readily did the Jewish Christians accept Gentiles, according to the story? How readily does the church accept new people today?
5. Choose a reporter who can recap the responses to these questions for the larger group.

Option B: Bring the dream and the parable home. Divide into two groups. One group will substitute names of real people for the characters in Jesus' parable (Luke 7:41-43). Rework the story and be prepared to present it to the whole group. The second group will substitute a real person and contemporary forbidden objects in Peter's dream (Acts 11:5-10). Rework the dream and be prepared to present it to the whole group. After the parable and dream have been presented, talk as a whole group.
1. Discuss the shock value in each case. Does a contemporary retelling have more shock value for you? Why or why not?
2. How convincing are these devices in getting people to change? Did it work in Bible times?
3. Peter and the Pharisee were both worried about would happen to the faith if just anybody was allowed in. What do you think happens when faith is open to everyone?
4. Recall stories of Ruth, Rahab, and Jonah and the Ninevites. How new is the idea of accepting outsiders for Peter and the Pharisee? What new thing do you think God is saying in Luke and Acts that hasn't been said before?

Respond (15 MINUTES)

Option A: Make a list of unspoken assumptions about membership in your congregation. For instance, does it matter what kind of clothes people wear? Can couples who are not married but living together be part of your congregation? Are bi-racial couples welcome? Are there certain beliefs and practices that are unacceptable in your group, such as universal restoration or women in leadership? Look over the list. Decide together which assumptions exclude certain people and which are hospitable and invite people to be included. Make a plan to be hospitable and break down barriers; for example, decide to have "dress down" Sundays to make people who dress very casually feel at home; or go as a group to visit a neighboring congregation very different from your own just for fellowship; or host a series of meals that draw in some unlikely guests.

Option B: Identify the hottest issue in the church today, one that could potentially split the church. If there is more than one issue, divide into groups with each group tackling a hot issue. Take turns telling how God speaks to you on the issue at hand. In what way is God saying a new thing? In what way is God saying an old thing? Come back together in the large group and recap the small group conversations.

Option C: Meet with your PEP. Join another pair if your partner is not present. Take turns sharing how God speaks to you and how you know God is actually speaking, and not just a temptation or rationalization. Individually complete this sentence starter on a card or slip of paper: "I know God has spoken to me when…" Lay your card in a pile in the center of the room and draw another person's. Then stand in a circle and take turns reading the cards to the group. Close by discussing whether things have changed very much since Peter's time in terms of faithful living, or whether things have stayed much the same. Why, in either case?

Closing (5 MINUTES)

Spend a moment of silence in which you thank God for the vision of Jesus and the courage of the early Christians who crossed cultural and religious boundaries to share the good news of God's love. Sing a unity hymn such as "Seed, Scattered and Sown" or "Come, Let Us All Unite to Sing."

PART III: LEADER GUIDELINES

Items Needed
Church directory
Paper and pens or markers
Bibles
Hymnals

Resources
Bernhard, Fred and Steve Clapp. *Widening the Welcome of Your Church.* LifeQuest, 1996.

Tips for Leading
1. Make a practice of reading through the entire session before leading the group. Choose the options you will use and think about how you would respond to the questions in the activities.
2. If members of the group are reticent to speak, be prepared to launch discussion by offering the first response.
3. Be aware of how the members of the group learn. Choose activities that will appeal to different styles. Some may like discussion, but others may like role playing, or prayer and singing. Be sure to do some of each in the time allotted. If, on the other hand, everyone unanimously likes discussion, use mostly stimulating questions and lively discussion starters.

Session 4
The Baby and the Bath Water

PART I: PREPARATION

Bible passages: Luke 13:10-17; Acts 5:12-32

Key verse: But Peter and the apostles answered, "We must obey God rather than any human authority" (Acts 5:29).

Summary: In a synagogue, a symbol of the Jewish status quo, Jesus liberates a woman from an affliction that has kept her bent over for 18 years. Authorities in the synagogue despise Jesus for what seems to them like endangerment. They think Jesus is threatening the very existence of the faith by dishonoring the law (in this case, healing on the Sabbath). Again in Acts, the apostles are healing on the steps of the temple against what amounted to a restraining order placed on them by temple authorities. But this time, to preserve the faith, the Sadducees and chief priests move quickly to arrest them and put them in a public jail. The apostles are liberated by an angel and return to the temple to heal. These two stories typify the conflict between Christians and Jews over interpretation of the faith. Jewish authorities labored under foreign occupation and fears of losing the faith if they weren't compliant. Jesus and the apostles, in the best tradition of Judaism, preached healing and liberation, convinced that God commanded them to do so, and since God was the true authority in their lives, they disregarded any human authority. We still struggle with these choices. Is it right to obey God even if we endanger the church or land in jail? And how do we know which issues are worth going to jail for, figuratively or literally? Should we preserve the church and its values at all costs, or should we preach the gospel even if the gospel creates conflict?

Study

It's a minor detail. Most of us miss it when we read the story of the woman stooped over. It seems of little consequence that this story in Luke takes place in a synagogue. It's not even the magnificent temple in Jerusalem, but a little synagogue in an outlying area. The synagogue may be a minor detail, but it has major importance.

The synagogue of Jesus' day is the refuge of Judaism in a country burdened under the foreign occupation of the Romans. The Romans tolerated Judaism and even allowed the Jews to maintain their own religious and political hierarchy to an extent, but Rome would have been just as glad to see the demise of Judaism. Jewish leaders struggled mightily to keep the faith. On one hand, they insisted on rigorous maintenance of Hebrew law and ritual purity to keep the embers of Israelite belief alive. On the other hand, they colluded with Roman authorities, mostly out of self-preservation. Go along to get along. They lived in a preservation mode.

It was against this background that Jesus' practice of healing on the Sabbath right in the synagogue looks so stark. By worship, rest, study, and refraining from work, Israel paused to remember that God, and not Rome, was taking care of them. It was the priest in the synagogue who taught the laws about the Sabbath, interpreted the law, and enforced it. He was the keeper of tradition and the heartbeat of the community. We often villainize Jewish leaders as being backward, mean, or corrupt, but in their defense it can be said that they were trying their hardest to preserve their lives and traditions. We might have done the same in their shoes. And we might even have honored them for defending the faith.

> Thou didst desire man's free love, that he should follow Thee freely, enticed and captivated by Thee. In place of the firm ancient law, man must hereafter with free heart decide for himself what is good and what is evil, having only Thy image before him as his guide. But did it not occur to Thee that he would at last question and indeed reject even Thy image and Thy truth, if he were weighed down with such a fearful burden as freedom of choice?
>
> —From "The Grand Inquisitor" in *The Brothers Karamazov*, by Fyodor Dostoevsky

Jesus comes from the very same tradition. He's also concerned about the faith. He is the fulfillment of all that Judaism has hoped for, for centuries. Perhaps he more than anyone is concerned for the future of the faith. He also thinks of the synagogue as the most appropriate place from which to interpret the laws and traditions of Judaism. But instead of being guarded and working out of a preservation mode, Jesus interprets

The Baby and the Bath Water

> Let the poor man's tears find more compassion in you, but not more justice, than the pleadings of the rich. Try to discover the truth behind the rich man's promises and gifts, as well as behind the poor man's sobbings and importunities…. If you should chance to bend the rod of justice, do not let it be with the weight of a bribe, but with that of pity.
>
> —Advice given to Sancho Panza by Don Quixote, in *Don Quixote* by Miguel de Cervantes

the laws to be liberating and freeing, just as they were for Hebrew slaves in Egypt and exiles in Babylon. In Luke 4:18-19 he has already proclaimed liberation and healing as his ministry, a ministry that fulfilled all the law and the prophets.

Luke uses many stories of conflict with Jewish leadership to set the scene for Jesus' execution and resurrection. Often the crowds are enthralled by Jesus' message while authorities stand in the background and grumble about Jesus. Something must be done about him, they say. Finally, after he persists in boldly preaching the good news (at one end of our bow tie), he completely irritates the authorities until they execute him (the knot of the bow tie). Jesus' death, in turn, leads ultimately to an explosion of new faith, healing, and liberation among Gentiles and Jewish Christians. In the end, ironically, the real preservation of the faith is apparently in its message of liberation and wholeness.

The apostles' ministry of healing

When we meet up with the apostles in Acts, they have taken up Jesus' ministry of liberation and healing in a charismatic way. Instead of roaming the countryside with the gospel, they are carrying it out on the temple steps in Jerusalem, right under the nose of Jewish and Roman authority. And the more active they become, the more the authorities retrench.

Temple leaders are not going to stand around and simply grumble about the growing Christian threat anymore. Christianity has somehow become even more threatening than Roman occupation. So if it means the Jewish authorities have to cooperate with Roman authorities to control the spread of Christianity, they will. The setting in Acts 5 is not only the temple. It is the temple and the jail—a Jewish institution and a Roman institution working together to contain the menace. When believers come in hordes and bring the sick on cots and lay them at the temple steps on mats, the temple police move in to arrest the apostles, putting them in a public prison.

A prison cannot hold the gospel of liberation and wholeness anymore than the tomb could contain Jesus. We see it later in Acts 16 when Paul and Silas are bound in jail for witnessing to the Lord. There a miraculous earthquake springs the doors open and they walk out—after converting the jailer to faith, that is! In the beginning God created the world by merely speaking it into being. When God said, "Let there be light," there was light. Now Jesus has come to proclaim good news to the poor, release to captives, sight for the blind, and freedom from oppression (Luke 4:18-19), and so it is. When people discover their freedom and value in Jesus Christ, they can no longer be kept from it, not by jails, or torture, or death.

The search for the apostles is downright comical. While temple police are on their way to fetch the apostles for trial, the apostles are already free, making their way back to the temple to continue their ministry. Then, as the authorities are standing around scratching their heads, trying to figure out what has happened, an unnamed person runs in with the embarrassing news that the apostles are back at it just outside on the temple steps. They rush out to capture them again and bring the apostles before the court. Just as Paul and Silas chose to remain in prison to confront the authorities, the apostles come before the council without a struggle. (As in many other situations, however, the temple authorities knew that the crowds outside were supportive of the apostles, and so they treated their captives with kid gloves so as not to arouse public anger.)

> The Fathers said: "Build a fence around the Torah" because a vineyard with a fence is safer than one without a fence. But a person should guard against building the fence too high, for then it may fall in and crush the plants it is supposed to guard.
>
> —Rabbi Nathan, Pirke Avot, in *The Word: A Spiritual Sourcebook*, by Noah benShea

At the hearing before the council, the apostles make a simple and brilliant defense: "We must obey God rather than human authority." It's the defense Daniel made to the court in Babylon. It's the proclamation that Joshua makes in Joshua 24:15 ("As for me and my household..."), forsaking all the competing religions and nations around him. It's the attitude Esther took in 4:16 when she had to go before the king to save the people of God ("I will go to the king, though it is against the law; and if I perish, I perish"). It's what the Jews in Jerusalem would like to have said to the Romans, but now that the apostles have upstaged them, the faithful response is a humiliating and impudent response to their authority.

The years under Roman rule were tough times for Israel, exiled in its own land and struggling against the odds to stay alive. In fact, Judaism nearly crumbled when the temple, the symbol of Jewish faith and teaching, was destroyed in about A.D. 70. It was a tough time for Christians, too. Stephen was martyred, Paul and Silas were beaten and jailed, and the seven churches of Asia Minor endured severe persecution. But the Christian cause was advancing nonetheless, perhaps because it gave hope in the midst of pain. As Paul testifies from prison, "I will continue to rejoice, for I know that through your prayers and the help of the Spirit of Jesus Christ this will turn out for my deliverance.... For to me, living is Christ and dying is gain" (Phil. 1:19-21). Casting the gospel as a gospel of liberation instead of preservation makes all the difference. Instead of fearing death, the gospel of liberation gives life and vitality. In it, we are all made new.

Things to think about: This week think about whether you are a person who likes to preserve things or pitch things. If you haven't already, plan to make a video or photographic inventory of your possessions for insurance purposes. If there were a natural disaster and these things were destroyed, which would you replace? Which would be impossible to replace? Which would not be worth replacing?

Talk with others this week about traditions and values that are important. How do you preserve them? Are traditions cumbersome for you or the source of joy? How do you establish new traditions?

There is renewed interest in keeping the Sabbath. Poll others about what they think we have lost by making the Sabbath the same as every other day.

PART II: THE SESSION

Focus (10 MINUTES)
After your usual opening, choose one of the following options to help the group focus on the session.

Option A: On a piece of paper, rank the following issues in the order in which you would be willing to go to prison or die to preserve. Your human rights, your civil rights, democracy, your faith, another faith, your children, your spouse, a neighbor, starving children in the world.

On a large sheet of newsprint with these issues written in large letters, note how many people said "human rights" was the number one issue for them. How many said "civil rights" was number one?— and so on down the list. If there is time, find out which item was last. What generalizations can you make about the values people cherish?

Transition: Both the Jewish leaders and the apostles of Jesus' time were willing to make sacrifices for faith. However, look at the texts to see how their approaches to save the faith took them in very different directions.

Option B: Have a time of confession: form two lines with equal numbers of people in each. Face the person directly across from you. In 20 seconds say what you like most about Christmas. Take another 20 seconds to hear what your partner likes most about Christmas. When the timekeeper says, "Change," take a step to the right and tell your new partner what you like about Christmas. Keep moving every 40 seconds until you have had four or five partners. Then repeat the exercise, except the second and fourth times around confess what you don't like about Christmas.

Transition: Sometimes traditions that are meant to help us celebrate Christ become overloaded with other meanings, interpretations, and expectations. At that point it's time to listen to God, who can remind us what is most important. See how the early Christians uncovered new meaning in the old story of faith that made their faith come alive.

Engage the Text (10 MINUTES)

Option A: Review the stories by acting them out. Choose parts and read them as a readers theater, or meet for a few minutes to decide how you will actually stage the two stories. Arrange chairs and tables to make a temple setting.

After you act out the stories, contrast how the temple leaders were portrayed with how Jesus was portrayed. With whom do you most identify and why? Now try some reverse thinking. What were the temple leaders doing right? What did Jesus do "wrong"? What dangerous risks were Jesus and the apostles taking? Realistically, if you were living under Roman occupation, would you comply or resist? Why?

How much healing and liberation takes place in these stories? How many fractures appear in the wider family of faith in these Scriptures? Which dominates, healing or conflict? Is it possible in these stories or in life to have healing without conflict? Why or why not?

Option B: Set the stage today. Listen as two volunteers read the stories from Luke and Acts. Notice that the temple is the setting for the stories in this session. It represents a number of things: authority, truth, and faith, to name a few. As a group, decide on the equivalent symbol in your community or country. What institution holds the most authority over you? Is it the church or some other institution? Take turns retelling the Bible stories, substituting in the story the most authoritative institution you can think of in your culture. When everyone who wishes has told a story, reflect together. What new insights did you gain from looking at the stories this way? What, if anything, surprises you?

Respond (20 MINUTES)

Option A: Apply the views of the temple leaders and Jesus to contemporary issues. In what ways do you think the traditional way is best and ought to be preserved in each case? In what ways should the church take a new look at these issues?
1. Women in ministry
2. Divorce and remarriage
3. Military service
4. Civil disobedience
5. The Ten Commandments
6. Other

Option B: Take turns sharing your plans for Sunday afternoon. List individuals' activities on a piece of newsprint or a chalkboard. Go back over the list as a group and try to reach consensus on how these activities fit the *spirit* of the law (Sabbath is for rest and renewal and liberation) and which of these activities fit the *letter* of the law (no work on the Sabbath).

Meet with your PEP to talk together about how you would adjust your plans for the day so that it is truly a renewing, relaxing day. Check with your PEP later to see if he or she was able to observe the Sabbath as Jesus taught.

Option C: Stand up for an issue. Jesus and the apostles practiced civil disobedience. The apostles even went to jail for the sake of the gospel. Divide into small groups of three or four people. Take turns telling what, if anything, you would be willing to go to prison for. In what way would your action bring liberation or healing to you and others? How would you gauge whether Jesus would have done the same?

When each has had a chance to share, rank the following authorities in the order that they rule in your life. Then share your rankings with others and discuss why you ranked them the way you did.
1. Jesus
2. The Bible
3. The state
4. God
5. Holy Spirit

Closing (5 minutes)

Say a prayer in unison: God of all power and authority, we thank you for the laws by which you have guided your people. And we thank you for Jesus, who came to make us free and whole. Grant us hearts and minds to see the life you offer us and the courage to follow no matter what. Amen.

Part III: Leader Guidelines

Items Needed
Newsprint or chalkboard
Pens and paper
Bibles

Tips for Leading
1. When talking about controversial topics, help participants honor and respect the views of others in the group. Open the session by reminding everyone that, while frank discussion is encouraged, critical comments aimed at people are inappropriate.
2. Keep discussion moving. Participants may get mired down on unsolvable issues. When the group gets stuck, move them onto another movement or topic.
3. At some point in the session, ask how the PEP partnerships are working. Suggest that the partnerships continue beyond this unit.
4. Read ahead to the next session. If necessary, tap several participants to take leadership in readers theater or other parts of the session. Their parts will come off more smoothly if they have advance notice and time for preparation.

Session 5

Let Us Pray

Part I: Preparation

Bible passages: Luke 5:12-17; Acts 9:10-19

Key verse: But he would withdraw to deserted places and pray (Luke 5:16).

Summary: Jesus heals a leper and then quickly retreats to solitude for prayer. Through prayer, Jesus renews himself after intense periods of ministry. But more importantly, Jesus uses prayer to reconnect himself to his Jewish roots and his life as the fulfillment of the messianic promise. With his past firmly established in Judaism, he faces his destiny, offering himself up to the world from the cross. Then in Acts, Paul is plunged into the solitude of blindness where he prays with Ananias. His prayers disconnect him from the past in which he persecuted Christians and establishes him as a minister of the gospel not only for his Jewish community, but for the world. For Jesus and Paul, prayer renews, connects, frees, and charges the body and soul for ministry. If prayer is so central to faith, can the Christian life be genuine without it?

Study

Woven through the chapters of Luke's books is Jesus' life of prayer. Dr. Huston Smith, author of *The World's Religions,* said once that the charisma of Jesus so evident to the crowds was directly related to the long hours he spent "soaking up divinity" in the quiet places. Jesus often prayed in solitude, but he also prayed the traditional prayers of Israel with others in the synagogue. The thing that makes Jesus' prayers distinctive is not the setting or the solitude; he prayed in synagogues and on hillsides, in public and in private. Jesus' prayers are distinctive because they connect Jesus with his ancestral past, revealing not only his Jewishness, but also his role as Messiah and the fulfillment in history of the messianic promise. As the fulfillment of God's plan for a messiah, however, Jesus must suffer on the cross, essentially alone as he is many times in prayer.

Luke's Gospel is composed of three main sections: the ministry in Galilee (4:14–9:50), in which Jesus establishes that he is the one sent from God to fulfill the law and the prophets; the journey to Jerusalem (9:51–19:48), where Jesus heads to his destiny; and the time in Jerusalem (20:1–23:56), when the prophecy is fulfilled. The first section is filled with prayer, both private and corporate; the second is filled with action and interaction, teaching and healing; and the third section returns to prayer. In the first and third sections, prayer alternates with action. Jesus' solitude is followed in most cases by interaction with large, clamoring crowds, and his identity as the Messiah is becoming ever more apparent, both to his fans and his detractors.

> Blessed art Thou, our Eternal God, Ruler of the Universe, Creator of the fruit of the vine. You have called us to holiness through your commandments. With love you gave us festivals for happiness, holidays for rejoicing, such as this time, the season of our freedom, the remembrance of the going out from Egypt.
>
> —a Seder prayer

Many of the prayer retreats are in the first section of Luke's Gospel. Each clearly connects Jesus to the Jewish messianic tradition and the mission for which God sent him. Note, for example, how he prays in a deserted place in 4:42, but when he returns, the crowds seek him out. He reminds them that "I must proclaim the good news of the kingdom of God to the other cities also; for I was sent for this purpose." Twice after spending time in prayer in the mountains, Jesus came down to face great multitudes of people. In 6:12 Jesus prays on the mountainside, then returns to call the 12 disciples, a connection to the 12 tribes of Israel. In 6:17 Jesus emerges from prayer to heal and cleanse people in the crowd, clearly the work of the "anointed one" of Jewish tradition as Jesus describes himself in Luke 4:18. Finally, Luke 9:37-43 follows the transfiguration where Jesus appears to Peter, John, and James as the Divine, that is, the Divine as it is known in the tradition of Moses and Elijah who are with the transfigured Jesus. This is another episode that connects Jesus to the Israelite messianic promise. After the transfiguration, Jesus returns from prayer to exorcize a demon from a child, an act that makes the crowds marvel at the greatness of God, for now they are beginning to understand that Jesus is the Messiah.

In the third section of Luke's Gospel, set in Jerusalem (20:1–23:56), three prayer events are recorded. The first is the Festival of Unleavened

Let Us Pray

Prayer of Abandonment
Father,
I abandon myself into your hands;
do with me what you will.
Whatever you may do, I thank you;
I am ready for all, I accept all.
Let only your will be done in me,
and in all your creatures—
I wish no more than this, Lord.
Into your hands I commend my soul;
I offer it to you with all the love of my heart,
for I love you, Lord,
and so need to give myself,
to surrender myself into your hands,
without reserve,
and with boundless confidence,
for you are my father.

—Brother Charles of Jesus

Bread, or the Passover, a celebration of the exodus from Egypt (22:1). The Passover meal, or Seder, is the central celebration of Jewish history, saturated with prayers that recall God's action to set Israel free. When Jesus blesses the cup and the bread (22:17, 19), he prays the prayers that have been passed down from generation to generation. Now he will be the one to deliver the people, to reconcile them to God. As the hour of the passion in Jerusalem draws close, Jesus' prayers prepare us for the inevitable—that Jesus must be sacrificed in order for the fulfillment to be complete.

The second prayer in the third section follows immediately. Jesus and the disciples withdraw to the garden on the Mount of Olives, a favorite place of prayer (22:39). Jesus prays, "Remove this cup from me; yet, not my will but yours be done" (22:42). No longer the prayer of the ancients, this is a personal plea for help, as well as a prayer of abandonment into the hands of God. Following this prayer another crowd gathers (22:47), though this was not the curious or sympathetic crowd drawn to Jesus in Galilee. Here the action turns sinister; "the power of darkness" is at work (22:53).

Jesus prays the third prayer from the cross. "Father, into your hands I commend my spirit" (23:46), a prayer of his ancestors from Psalm 31:5. The final prayer of his earthly life is at once his most personal prayer yet also one woven inextricably into the history of Israel. The magnificently mysterious action of the cross concludes, on Jesus' part, with this prayer. His role, which has been developing all along, is now focused, as it were, like the knot of the bow tie, in his single solitary moment on the cross. It all comes down to this, that the Savior will become an example for others and will be sacrificed so that others can live. The prayers have been pointing all along to a messiah who was sent not to save in life, but by death. Those who were looking for a political messiah to deliver them in this life unwittingly execute Jesus, fulfilling God's plan that Jesus will unleash the forces of faith on the world.

Prayer in Acts

Prayer in Luke connects Jesus to the past and leads to the present fulfillment of the messianic prophecy. Then in Acts, prayer disconnects the faith from Judaism alone and opens faith to the world. Gathered in Jerusalem, the disciples and the women who follow Jesus devote themselves to prayer (Acts 1:14). But as the church grows, the believers pray together in their homes (2:42), moving beyond the synagogue as the place of prayer and tradition. While Jesus' followers continue to worship in the temple as often as possible (2:46), they begin to pray wherever the faithful are gathered—in homes, by the water, on ships, and on the road.

Peter, devout Jew that he is, goes to the roof to pray in Acts 10:9. He has chosen a place set apart. When he is withdrawn and in prayer, he receives a message from the God of the Jews that frees him from the past traditions of Israel and prods him to move out and engage the Gentile world in faith. Read that sentence again and ponder the profound change this dream represents. Through prayer, Peter gains the freedom to go out from his past, which was exclusively for the people of Israel, and gives the liberating, healing Word of God to everybody who will accept it. That's an enormous turning point in the New Testament.

> It is essential, I maintain, to begin the practice of prayer with a firm resolution to persevere in it.
>
> —St. Teresa, *Way of Perfection*

Saul's prayer is also uttered in solitude, but a solitude of a different kind! The former persecutor of Christians is struck blind and is forced into a solitariness that produced miraculous "insight." In his blindness, Paul also comes to the realization that faith is the destiny for Gentiles, which, in biblical terms, means practically the known world.

Following his conversion, Paul is a man of action, but he also remains a man of prayer. As a Pharisee, he frequents synagogues (Acts 13:5, 14; 14:1; 17:1-3; 18:4; 19:8) where he, like Jesus and Peter, prays the Psalms. Where there is no Jewish settlement large enough to support a synagogue, he goes to places where folks gather to pray (16:13). That Christians began to pray and meet outside the synagogue indicates that the tradition that bore Jesus and connected us to the God of the Israelites is no longer exclusive. It quickly becomes the "tradition" of many.

Let Us Pray

> There is no contradiction between action and contemplation when Christian apostolic activity is raised to the level of pure charity. On that level, action and contemplation are fused into one entity by the love of God and of our brother in Christ. But the trouble is that if prayer is not itself deep, powerful and pure and filled at all times with the spirit of contemplation, Christian action can never really reach this high level.
>
> —Thomas Merton, *Contemplative Prayer*

To say that Peter and Paul disconnect from their past and are freed to go beyond it is perhaps too strong. The early Christian movement did not forsake the past. They were still the people of the God of Abraham, Isaac, and Jacob. They were very much the people of God's saving acts. They were the people of the Messiah and people of the promise. And they were a people of prayer. Instead of getting free of their past, they were freed in prayer to open the past to everyone. In those reflective moments between hectic missionary efforts, they refreshed themselves with the graceful, welcoming voice of their ancestral God and the God of their descendants near and far.

Things to think about: Find time in your busy week to reconnect with God in prayer. Try different ways of praying, such as reading prayers, speaking your own prayers, singing, confessing, and praying prayers of gratitude. Which kind of prayer helps you connect with God best? How does prayer challenge you?

How balanced is your life between prayer and action? Check with others in your household, your school, or your workplace. What is the "right" combination of prayer and action?

Part II: Session

Focus (10 minutes)

After the usual session opening, choose one of the following options to focus on the topic.

Option A: Do a quick inventory of the amount of time you spend in prayer each week and how much time you spend in other activities. On a sheet of paper, draw a vertical scale, the top being 100%, the bottom being 0%. Mark what percent of the week you spend in prayer. Also mark the percentage of time you spend sleeping, working, and in non-work activities. Then share your scale with the group if you wish. What does prayer do for you personally? Which is more difficult for you, prayer or action? In what ways are they the same?

Option B: Take turns reciting childhood prayers you learned for bedtime and mealtime. What do these prayers do for children? for adults? Should kids learn to pray at a young age? Why or why not?

Option C: When should you pray? And how often? Choose a bead from an old necklace. Keep it in your pocket and pray as you turn it over and over in your fingers. If time permits, make a prayer bead from modeling clay that can be dried or baked.

Transition: We often focus on the sayings and ministry of Jesus, but Jesus also had a prayer life. He often retreated for prayer between tense periods of ministry. Look at passages in Luke and Acts that show what part prayer played in the mission work of Jesus and the apostles.

Engage the Text (20 MINUTES)

Option A: Make Scripture sandwiches. Divide into groups of three people. Take one of the following Scriptures on meditation and read it together as a small group. Then have one person in the group find out what happened immediately before the assigned Bible verse and the third person in the group find out what happened immediately after. Return to the large group. Take turns standing as a small group, sandwiching the person who read the assigned text on meditation between the people who researched the situation before and after. Report on your text (before, during, and after meditation). In what ways does the story of meditation connect Bible characters with their roots and where does their ministry go from there?
Luke 4:42
Luke 6:12
Luke 9:37
Acts 9:10-11
Acts 10:9

Option B: Listen as someone reads Luke 4:40-44. Then take part in a role play that includes Jesus and the crowd. Have those who are playing people in the crowd descend on Jesus with requests for healing. The person playing Jesus will try to handle as many cases as possible in five minutes. Close the role play, listening as the narrator reads verses 42-44 again.

Discuss what it must have been like for Jesus, battling big crowds with serious problems. How did the actor who played Jesus feel about the onslaught? How do you imagine the people in the crowd felt? In what ways can you identify with their sense of emergency? In the face of so much need, how does Jesus' reason for moving on sound to crowd members? to the actor who played Jesus?

Respond (20 MINUTES)

Option A: Try a different style of prayer called the *Lectio Divina*. This is an ancient Christian discipline used to pray the Scriptures. *Lectio Divina* begins by quietly asking God to speak through Scripture. After growing silent, read a brief passage of Scripture. This might be something from the Psalms, a parable or teaching of Jesus, or another familiar passage. Read the passage slowly several times. Note the images or phrases that "pop out." Close your eyes and hold that image or phrase in your mind and let your mind move into your heart. Wait and see what happens as you hold what God has given you. After several minutes of quietly waiting on God with that image in mind, close with a prayer of thanksgiving.

Or try memorizing a Psalm. If everyone agrees on memorizing the same short Psalm, you can help one another recite it from memory at the end of 10 or 15 minutes.

Those who prefer to write, may write a prayer. Try to connect yourself to God and offer yourself to be a light for the world, modeling your prayer after the prayers of Jesus, Peter, and Paul.

Option B: Take this time to meet with your PEP (Partners Encouraging Perseverance) to talk about the balance of prayer and action in your life. If you haven't already, briefly inventory your time during the week to see how much time you give to renewal and how much time you are active and working. Share your time inventory with your PEP. Make plans for how you will bring more balance between your prayer and work life.

Closing (5 MINUTES)

Hold hands in a circle. Spend a minute in silence. Allow time for personal prayer. Close by reading or reciting Psalm 23 in unison.

PART III: LEADER GUIDELINES

Items Needed
Paper
Pens or pencils

Bibles
Beaded necklace or modeling clay

Resources
Foster, Richard J. *Prayer: Finding the Heart's True Home.* Harper S.F., 1992.

Tips for Leading
1. Prayer is personal. Many people struggle with prayer and may fear being honest about their struggle. To encourage open and honest sharing, remind individuals that what is said in class is to be treated with complete confidentiality.
2. Emphasize that balance is not necessarily a question of equality but a question of "enoughness." That is, some people may pray a little but not enough in the scope of a day or week. Some people may pray less than half of their waking hours, but that may be too much, especially if they pray earnestly but are never motivated to act. Help people think about striking the correct balance in their lives between connecting to God and connecting to the world, whatever that may be.
3. Broaden the concept of prayer for those who think they don't like to pray. Help them to see that, at times, daily routines, loving their children, studying the Bible, and other actions are ways of connecting with God, i.e., ways of "prayer."

Session 6
A Gift: Count the Cost

PART I: PREPARATION

Bible passages: Luke 6:46-49; Acts 2:40-47

Key verse: "Why do you call me 'Lord, Lord,' and do not do what I tell you? (Luke 6:46)."

Summary: Eager crowds collect around Jesus to hear his teachings, but few take up the difficult life of discipleship he sets before them. By the time Jesus is crucified, the throng has dwindled to almost no one. He is alone at the cross. But in Acts, the Holy Spirit breathes life into converts and thousands are saved. The new-found zeal for discipleship might have disappeared after the initial thrill of the coming of the Holy Spirit, except that believers quickly formed the church and instituted a tradition of community life, prayer, worship, and care for others, sustaining their enthusiasm for the long haul. In what ways does the church community help you be a better disciple? Is it possible to be a disciple without the church?

Study

Jesus was a popular rabbi. Large, curious crowds gathered around him as he taught and healed in Galilee. People were eager to learn from both the example of his life and his strange teachings. The 12 disciples formed an inner circle, but there were many others who followed Jesus, including a group of women who supported the 12 and Jesus. Together these men and women were a band of travel companions for Jesus, as well as his students. Not only did they follow Jesus to learn from him, they crossed over the student/teacher line to walk beside Jesus as his friends. So when Jesus calls Levi to a life of discipleship (Luke 5:27), he "invites" him into a relationship as companion rather than mere student.

The Latin root of the word *companion* is the word for bread—*pan*. *Com* is the prefix meaning "with." So a companion is someone with whom we eat, someone with whom we live or commune. No wonder Jesus' teachings come to us in the form of stories about eating with people or attending great feasts. To take up the life Jesus offers to his disciples means sharing a table with outcasts and eating on the Sabbath. In both the spiritual sense and the literal sense, these acts of discipleship were dangerous and difficult for Jews in Jesus' time.

Disciples then, as disciples now, had difficulty both with carrying out the mandates of discipleship and with facing the consequences when they did. Who wouldn't? It's difficult to see what we're getting when we give up everything in the material world to follow Christ. It's hardly enticing to think of the sick and the lame and the demon-possessed as neighbors. No one is terribly excited about letting tomorrow take care of itself just because the flowers and birds don't worry about the future. And very few people are interested in breaking the law to be faithful to the gospel. Jesus no doubt knew that discipleship wasn't going to be popular. His question in Luke 6:46 is rhetorical. He knows the answer.

> But the medium is Christ whom no one can truly know unless he follows him in his life, and no one may follow him unless he has first known him.... For whoever thinks he belongs to Christ must walk the way that Christ walked.
>
> —Hans Denck, "The Contention that Scripture Says," in *Anabaptism in Outline*

Jesus' following dwindles until he is alone on the cross. Only the Roman centurion stands with him, an unlikely disciple. In one last aspect, we see the shape of the Gospel and Acts taking the shape of a bow tie. The crowds come to nothing at the crucifixion. It's not until Pentecost when the Holy Spirit rushes in and thousands are saved that we see a revival among believers and scads of new converts. From here the bow tie broadens to include many disciples, living the faith with zeal.

Thriving on the enthusiasm with which they converted, the new Christians in Jerusalem take Jesus' invitation to heart. They sell everything they have and distribute wealth or goods to people who need it. They live together and share everything in common. They pray and study together in the temple, and they eat together, breaking bread to remember Jesus. Nothing they do is easier than it was in Jesus' time. It's still dangerous to be a Christian. It's still hard to be selfless. It's still a challenge to believe. So why is the church in Acts able to convert disciples in great numbers when Jesus, the Master Teacher and Savior, could only attract a few?

One of the answers is community. Not only is there safety in numbers, there is encouragement. Before Paul arrives on the scene and talks about

A Gift: Count the Cost

the "body" of Christ with its combined talents that are stronger than the limited talents of a single person, Luke is already suggesting that discipleship is a community matter. Jesus puts the charge to many individuals who shrink from the lonely challenge of discipleship, but the converts in Jerusalem pool their resources and help each other along in both the spiritual disciplines and the disciplines of compassion.

> The Disciplines are best exercised in the midst of our normal daily activities. If they are to have any transforming effect, the effect must be found in the ordinary junctures of human life: in our relationships with our husband or wife, our brothers and sisters, our friends and neighbors.
>
> —From *Celebration of Discipline* by Richard J. Foster

Discipleship today

The early church provides a model for discipleship today. They studied together. They spent time together in fellowship. They shared communion. They prayed together. Likewise, the network of churches that was established after the persecution in Jerusalem shows how mutual support not only among individual followers, but also among congregations, helped Christians remain faithful in the face of difficulty. Discipleship is an individual choice. But it is always within the context of a community, and from there a web of communities.

Disciplines are called disciplines because they are difficult. It would be easier if we didn't need to set aside time in our busy schedules to pray. Things would be simpler if we never had to offer hospitality to folks who have been strangers or enemies. Precisely because it is such hard work, disciples are never asked to go it alone. They are set within a community that provides encouragement. An increasing number of Christians are adopting the ancient practice of finding a spiritual director who can help them fulfill the disciplines to which they are called.

The power of the Pentecost might have fizzled and the zeal of the first Christian converts might have waned if the church hadn't appeared. As people coalesced into congregations, traditions of the eucharist, the agape meal, worship, and music, to name a few, began to appear. These disciplines helped to regularly renew the zeal that the converts first experienced at Pentecost and to sustain the energy for living out the Christian faith. Now, two millennia later, congregational life still energizes us for discipleship. Collective worship inspires us, collective wisdom guides us, and collective compassion enables us to serve many. In biblical economics, the cost of discipleship is still high, but the returns on living the Christian life are out of this world.

Session 6

Things to think about: Literally figure the cost of discipleship for yourself or your family this week. Sit down and figure what it would cost you financially to "follow" Jesus as you understand it. Would following Jesus mean giving up your job, for instance? Would it mean living somewhere else? Would it mean giving away your things? Or figure out what you would make if you sold everything. Then figure how far your earnings would go toward helping others.

Talk with your spouse, family, co-workers, or friends this week about discipleship. How do they balance the personal discipline of prayer with the discipline of compassion? What, if any, is the right balance?

PART II: SESSION

Focus (10 MINUTES)

After the group's usual opening, choose an activity to focus on the session.

Option A: Use some or all of the following discussion starters.
1. I've been a parent for 15 years. Some days I wonder why I got myself into this, but I go on because…
2. I've been doing the same job now for years. I would quit and go somewhere else to work, but…
3. We've lived in the same town and the same house since our children were small. We've talked about moving but we've decided to stay because…
4. My congregation is small, so everybody has to serve on a committee. Seems like I've done church work for a hundred years, but I keep doing it because…

> Those who fear to see too clearly what this love asks, fool themselves by thinking that they have this watchful and devoted love. There is only one way to love God: to take not a single step without him, and to follow with a brave heart wherever [God] leads.
>
> —From *Christian Perfection* by Francois Fenelon

Option B: Look how far you've come. Subtract 10 years from your age. Ten years ago, what did you think you would be doing today? Write your memory on a card without signing your name. Pile the cards in the middle of the room. Pick someone else's card and mill around the room asking questions to find the owner of the card.

When all the cards are returned to their owners, talk about how easy or difficult it is to stay on track with dreams and plans. How can it be accomplished? What stands in the way?

A Gift: Count the Cost

What you need to do, then, dear Christian, if you are in bondage in the matter of service, is to put your will over completely into the hands of our Lord.... I have seen this done often in cases where it looked beforehand an utterly impossible thing. In one case, where a lady had been for years rebelling fearfully against a little act of service which she knew was right, but which she hated, I saw her, out of the depths of despair, and without any feeling whatever, give her will in that matter up into the hands of her Lord, and begin to say to Him, "Thy will be done; Thy will be done." And in one sweet hour that very thing began to look sweet and precious to her.

— From *The Christian's Secret of a Happy Life* by Hannah Whithall Smith

Option C: Take turns naming projects you started with great energy and never completed.

Transition: We often have dreams, hopes, ideas, and energy for great things, but when we get down in the trenches, it's hard to sustain our zeal. The same might have been true for early Christians after the resurrection and the Pentecost. Luke gives us insight into how Christians maintained their zeal and how we can experience the same energy today.

Engage the Text (20 MINUTES)

Option A: Read some texts that define what it means to be a follower of Jesus. As someone reads the following texts from Luke, listen carefully for requirements you could or couldn't abide. Mark them with a pencil if you're reading along. When each text is read a second time, stand or raise your hand when you think you would have to say no to following Christ.
Luke 6:46-49
Luke 12:22-34
Luke 14:25-33
Luke 18:18-25

After you have heard the texts, discuss the following questions:
1. Why would anyone want to be a disciple as Jesus has defined discipleship?
2. What are the rewards of discipleship according to these passages?
3. What is the least that someone could do to be a disciple? the most?
4. What do you think would have happened to Jesus' following if the Holy Spirit had not descended on the church in Jerusalem?
5. What did happen to the church when the Holy Spirit descended on it as reported in Acts 2?

Option B: How did they keep on keeping on? Listen as someone reads Acts 2:40-47. Mark in your Bible the disciplines that the early church practiced, for example, studying the apostles' teachings, gathering in fellowship, breaking bread and praying together, holding possessions in common, giving to the poor, eating meals together, and worshiping.

In your Bible, pencil in the contemporary equivalents of these disciplines, such as Sunday school and communion. Read the passage again with the contemporary practices. Then discuss the following questions:
1. How do the traditions of the church inspire you? How do they refresh the congregation?
2. How does your congregation practice each of these disciplines today?
3. At what level should we be able to sustain the congregation's zeal for discipleship? A high level? A low but steady level? Why?
4. To what extent is it better to share some things in common, for example, over a long period, rather than demand that everyone share everything right off the bat?
5. How do you think the rich ruler in Luke 18 would have fared in the church in Acts 2? Would the church have helped or hindered him from becoming a disciple? Why?

Respond (15 MINUTES)

Option A: Work at a definition of discipleship. Based on what you have read in Luke and Acts, write a definition of discipleship for yourself. If you wish, share your definition with the group.

Option B: Give a testimony. If you are led, tell others in the group why you belong to a church community. What part does the church play in your discipleship? Why do you prefer a church setting in which to practice faith over a personal faith that relies on private study and discipline?

Meet briefly with your PEP. Talk about ways you can encourage each other in your discipleship. Make a plan to follow through on encouraging each other.

Option C: Disciples have always struggled to be faithful to their call. Disciplines are gifts that open us to the gift of God's power. Through disciplines we try to align ourselves with God's work in the world. Some of the disciplines listed in Acts 2 are disciplines that are practiced together: study, fellowship, communion, and prayer. Which disciplines are you currently practicing and find helpful? Spend some time as a class sharing your "success stories."

Closing (5 MINUTES)

Because this is the last session, take a few minutes to share what have been for you the high points in Luke and Acts. What one thing will you take from this time together that has enriched your faith and work as a follower of Jesus? Also share anything that is still troubling you.

Close by standing in a circle, joining hands, and praying together the Lord's Prayer.

PART III: LEADER GUIDELINES

Items Needed
Index cards
Pens or pencils
Bibles

Resources
Bonhoeffer, Dietrich. *The Cost of Discipleship.* Touchstone Books, 1995.
Foster, Richard J. *Celebration of Discipline*, rev. ed. Harper S.F., 1988.

Tips for Leading
1. Be sure to allow time at the end of the session to review the six-week study of Luke and Acts. Use the evaluation form at the back of this book as a way to review the unit.
2. Remember that everyone falls short of being a perfect disciple. Assure people that they can still be disciples of Jesus even if they are not perfect. At the same time, challenge people to strive for more than just an "adequate" response to Jesus' call to follow.
3. Talk about what the group will study following this unit. Make sure everyone has access to the study material.